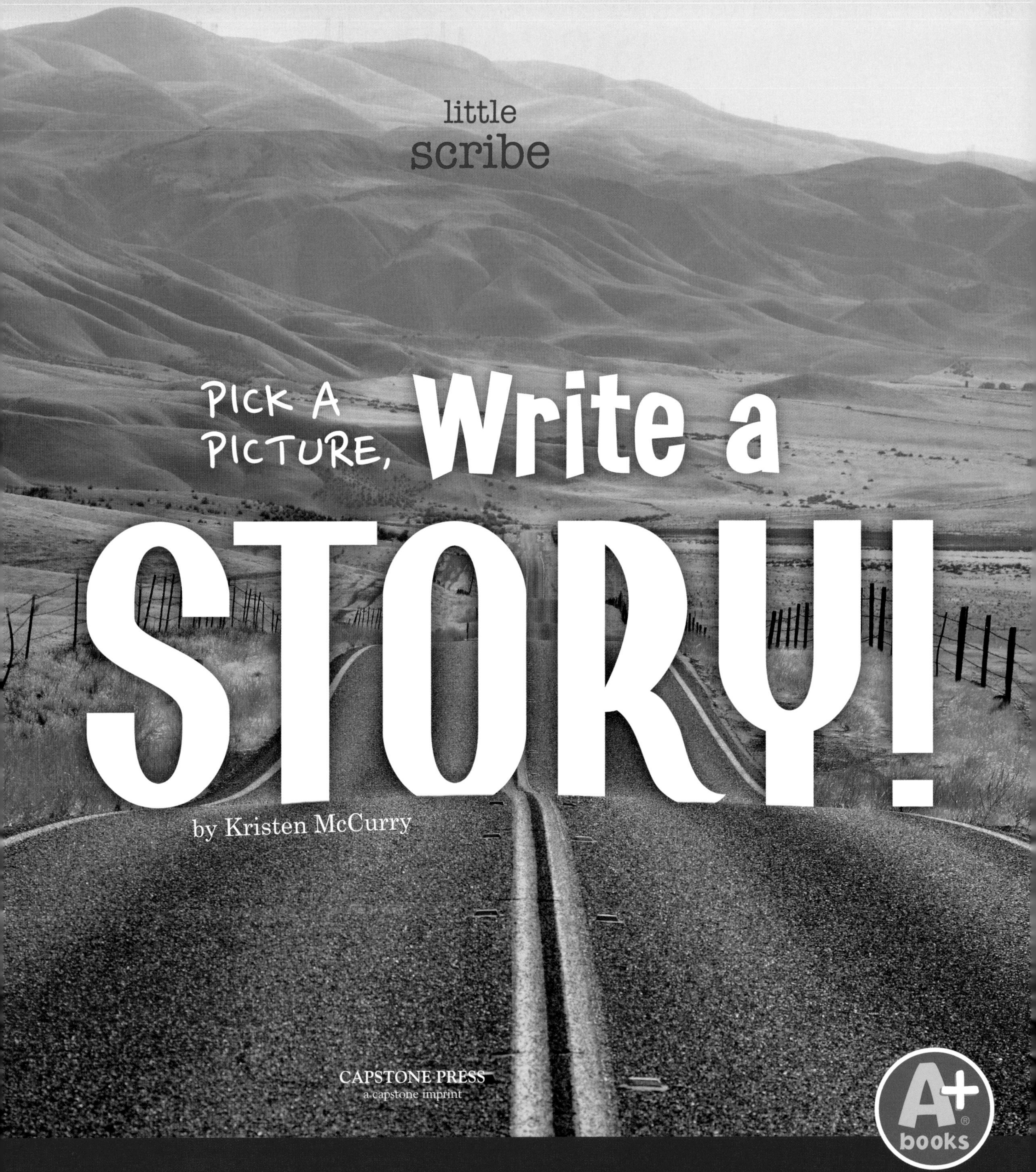

little
scribe

PICK A PICTURE, Write a STORY!

by Kristen McCurry

CAPSTONE PRESS
a capstone imprint

A+
books

A+ Books are published by Capstone Press,
1710 Roe Crest Drive, North Mankato, Minnesota 56003
www.capstonepub.com

For Soren. —KM

Library of Congress Cataloging-in-Publication Data
McCurry, Kristen.
Pick a picture, write a story! / by Kristen McCurry.
pages cm. — (A+Books: Little Scribe)
 Summary: "Introduces fiction story writing to children using photographs as idea prompts"— Provided by publisher.
 Audience: Ages 5-8
 ISBN 978-1-4765-4238-6 (library binding)
 ISBN 978-1-4765-5105-0 (paperback)
 ISBN 978-1-4765-5950-6 (eBook PDF)
1. Fiction—Authorship—Juvenile literature. 2. Short story—Authorship—Juvenile literature. 3. Photographs—Juvenile literature. 4. Child authors. I. Title.
PN3373.M37 2014
808.3'1—dc23   2013032324

Thanks to our adviser for her expertise, research, and advice:
Kelly Boswell, reading consultant and literacy specialist

Editorial Credits
Kristen Mohn, editor; Heidi Thompson, designer; Danielle Ceminsky, production specialist

Photo Credits
iStockphotos: Antrey, cover, 10, technotr, 27; Shutterstock: 1000 Words, 5, Alexander Ishchenko, 18-19, atikinka, 22-23, Cyril Hou, 17, James Mattil, 28, jordache, 20-21, kavram, 1, Lenkadan, 26, Melissa Hanes, 24, Natali Glado, 17 (inset), oliveromg, 14-15, otsphoto, 12-13, PerseoMedusa, 7, Tsekhmister, 8-9, Zurijeta, 30

Note to Parents, Teachers, and Librarians
This Little Scribe book uses full color photographs and a nonfiction format to introduce the concept of writing stories. *Pick a Picture, Write a Story!* is designed to be read aloud to a pre-reader or to be read independently by an early reader. Photographs help listeners and early readers understand the text and concepts discussed. The book encourages further learning by including the following sections: Table of Contents, Glossary, Read More, Critical Thinking Using the Common Core, and Internet Sites. Early readers may need assistance using these features.

Printed in the United States of America in Stevens Point, Wisconsin.
092013   007773WZS14

Table of Contents

What Is a Story? 4

Finish the Story 6

Borrow a Story 8

A Different Point of View 11

Characters Are Key 12

Plot Your Path 14

Up for a Challenge? 16

Picture the Setting 18

Putting It Together 20

Dialogue Is Talk! 22

Kinds of Stories 24

Action! 26

Brainstorming 29

Glossary 31

Read More 31

Critical Thinking Using the
Common Core 32

Internet Sites 32

What Is a Story?

A story is a narrative. It's a series of events told in order from beginning to end. Think about a joke or a riddle. If you tell the ending first, it's not as funny!

Stories are fun to hear and fun to tell. They are also fun to write! Stories usually tell about events that are make-believe—they didn't really happen.

Words and Pictures

You can write words and draw pictures to help tell your stories. A teacher can help you with your writing.

You can use photos to get ideas for stories. This photo makes a good story starter. Maybe the dog is on an adventure. Or maybe he's being rescued. Those are both great story ideas.

What do you think is happening?
Write down what you imagine.
That's a story.

Finish the Story

Here's the beginning of a story about some puppets that come to life at night.

At last the sun went down. The shopkeeper hung up the closed sign, locked the door, and left. Peter Puppet looked around. The people were all gone.

"Wake up, everyone! It's safe!" he called to the other toys.

How would you finish the story? Make a list of the different things that could happen.

Beginning, Middle, and End

Part of the Story	Peter Puppet Story
The **beginning** usually introduces who the story is about. It might also tell where and when the story takes place.	**Who:** Peter Puppet and his friends **Where and When:** a toyshop at night
The **middle** tells the action. Maybe there is a problem to be solved. Maybe there is a mystery or a question that needs answering.	**What:** This story might tell about a missing toy that the others must help find.
The **end** of a story is the answer to the question, "What happened?" How was the mystery or problem solved?	**How or Why:** Was the missing toy found in a funny place? How did it get there? How did the friends find it?

Borrow a Story

A good way to practice story writing is to borrow one you already know. Then change the story to make it your own. *The Three Little Pigs* is a well-known story. What if you made it more about the wolf than the pigs? You could explain why the wolf was chasing the pigs. Or maybe the wolf is the hero in your story!

Who's Telling the Story?

When a character is telling the story, it's called a **first-person** story.	<u>I</u> huffed and <u>I</u> puffed and <u>I</u> blew the house down!
When a narrator or storyteller is telling the story, it's called a **third-person** story.	<u>The wolf</u> huffed and <u>he</u> puffed and <u>he</u> blew the house down!

A Different Point of View

Imagine what it's like to be someone—or something—else. The world would look very different from other points of view.

Imagine you are the bug in this photo. What do you think it would feel like to be so small? Write about what you would see and feel from the bug's point of view.

Characters Are Key

It's hard to tell a story without characters. Characters are people or animals in your story. You might have only one character or many characters. A character can be brave or weak, small or big. You get to decide what your characters are like!

Write about a kitten … a kitten who thinks she's a tiger! You can give her a name and write other details about her. What does she like to do? What does she want more than anything? What makes your character special? Interesting characters help build interesting stories.

Plot Your Path

A picture shows one moment in time. But a story is not just one moment. A story is many moments together that change the character. Those moments or events are called the plot. The plot is the path a story takes.

Look at this photo, and then let your imagination take over. What led up to this moment? What happens next?

Building a Plot

Make a list of what you want to happen in your story. It can help you build a plot. Here's an example:

1. A boy is chasing a butterfly.

2. He looks down and sees that the ground has disappeared.

3. The boy discovers that he can fly!

Come up with
one or more plot
ideas for a story.
What happens
to the boy?

Up for a Challenge?

A challenge is a problem or task your character might face. Thinking about a challenge is a good way to come up with a plot idea.

Looking at these two pictures of birds might give you a plot idea.

What if a bird with this beak ...

wished he had this beak?

Write a story about the bird and the different ways he tries to change his beak. Does it work? What happens at the end?

Picture the Setting

The setting is where a story is "set"—where it takes place. Including details about the setting makes your story feel real. Imagine you are there and describe everything you can.

I shivered in the cool, silent forest. It was so dark that I stumbled on a root and fell. My hands and knees sank into the soft, mossy ground. As I got up, I saw a soft glow ahead. Was that a light?

Use Your Senses

Picture yourself in the setting. Think about what you would see, hear, smell, feel, or even taste. Paint a picture with words for your readers so they can imagine what you imagine.

Write more about the setting of this photo and what happens to the character as she makes her way toward the light.

Putting It Together

This picture makes a great story starter. It has a character and a setting. What story would you write about a guinea pig at the library? Does he want to learn to read? Imagine how the library would look and feel and smell to a guinea pig. Include those details in your story.

Dialogue Is Talk!

When your characters speak, it's called dialogue. Often you will see their words in quotation marks. Dialogue is a tool that can help move the story along. It can also provide details about the characters. How would they talk? What would they say?

"Hello!" said the girl.

"Woof!" said the dog.

That's dialogue!

Write some dialogue between this girl and the dog. Use your imagination to come up with something funny she might be saying. Does the dog answer her?

23

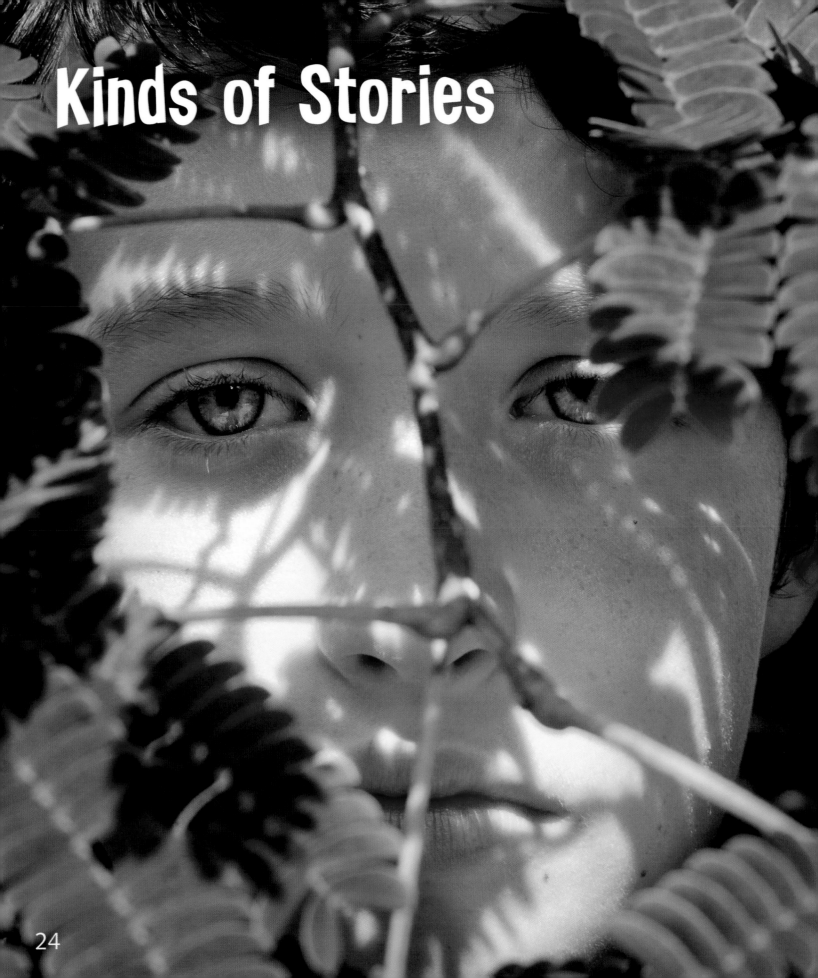

Kinds of Stories

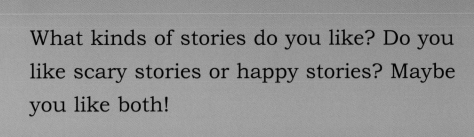

What kinds of stories do you like? Do you like scary stories or happy stories? Maybe you like both!

Common Kinds of Stories

Mystery	a story about a crime or other problem to be solved
Fairy Tale	a magical story that often has a happy ending
Fantasy	a story with strange and magical characters and places
Science Fiction	a fantasy story that takes place in an imaginary time or place—often about space travel, aliens, or robots
Adventure	a story about a character who must find or do something difficult on a journey

A story can be more than one kind. You might have a fairy tale in which the characters go on an adventure. Or a story might be a mystery with a science fiction setting. It can be fun to mix up types of stories to make yours just the way you want it.

What or who do you think this boy is hiding from? What type of story would you write about this picture?

Action!

Ajax reared up on his hind legs. He batted Triton with his front legs. Suddenly Ajax felt a sharp pain. Triton's teeth sank into his neck. Then Ajax heard a loud squeal. It was coming from him!

Action keeps a story moving. Maybe your character is being chased by a bear. Or maybe she is in a race and another runner is right on her heels. Exciting details in your story will make your readers want to know what happens next!

Your turn! Write an action scene about this photo.

Brainstorming

Brainstorming means to use your imagination to come up with ideas. Photos are a great place to start.

Here's a picture of an unusual building. What happened to it? Did it melt? Come up with a list of five different reasons the building looks this way. Add details to each reason. One of those ideas might turn into a story!

Story ideas are everywhere. Look through a book or magazine to find photos that spark story ideas for you. If you need help getting started, ask your teacher.

The most important thing is to keep writing. The more you write, the better you will get. And don't forget to keep reading too. Reading great stories is a good way to learn to write them. Soon your friends and family will be asking when they can read your next story.

Glossary

brainstorm—to think of many ideas without judging them as good or bad

challenge—something that is hard to do

character—a person or creature in a story

detail—a piece of information; a small part of a bigger thing

dialogue—the words spoken between two or more characters

event—a thing that happens

first-person—telling a story from a personal viewpoint; first-person writing uses personal words such as I, me, and we

hero—someone who has courage, strength, and does things that other people can't do

introduce—to bring in something new

narrative—an account of something that has happened

narrator—a person who tells a story or describes an event

plot—what happens in a story

point of view—eyes through which a story is told

quotation marks—a pair of punctuation marks that go around spoken words

setting—the time and place of a story

third-person—viewpoint that describes the events of a story through one character's eyes

Read More

Ganeri, Anita. *Animal Stories*. Writing Stories. Chicago: Heinemann Library, 2013.

Manushkin, Fran. *What Happens Next, Katie? Writing a Narrative with Katie Woo*. Katie Woo, Star Writer. North Mankato, Minn.: Picture Window Books, 2014.

Minden, Cecilia, and Kate Roth. *How to Write a Mystery*. Language Arts Explorer Junior. Ann Arbor, Mich.: Cherry Lake Pub., 2013.

Critical Thinking Using the Common Core

Study the chart on page 6. Think of a story you know, and make a chart showing the beginning, middle, and end of that story. (Integration of Knowledge and Ideas)

Look at the information about challenges on page 16. Then explain what challenge the bird on page 17 faces. (Craft and Structure)

Look at the Common Kinds of Stories chart on page 25. Then read the story passage about the horses on page 26. Which kind of story do you think this might be? (Key Ideas and Details)

Internet Sites

FactHound offers a safe, fun way to find Internet sites related to this book. All of the sites on FactHound have been researched by our staff.

Here's all you do:

Visit *www.facthound.com*

Type in this code: 9781476542386

 Check out projects, games and lots more at **www.capstonekids.com**